To

_____

From

_____

Let go

60 Powerful Truths to Set Your Heart Free

KATY FULTS

Let Go: 60 Powerful Truths to Set Your Heart Free
© 2019 Katy Fults All rights reserved.
First Edition, August 2019

Published by:

DaySpring

P.O. Box 1010
Siloam Springs, AR 72761
dayspring.com

Written by Katy Fults
Hand-lettered by Katy Fults
Designed and Typeset by Hannah Skelton
Printed in China
Prime: 94333
ISBN: 9781644543047

Contents

Introduction

Hello! I'm Katy. I am a wife, mom, painter, designer, and huge dreamer. I love books, paintbrushes, daisies, chips and guacamole, and sunsets with pink clouds. My life is full, chaotic, fun, and so, so amazing. But it is not perfect. In fact, a lot of days, it's pretty messy. Really messy.

I learned awhile back that we have a choice in how we choose to live. We can pretend like we have it all together, like we know exactly what we're doing and all of our ducks are in a row. Or we can choose to live authentically. To be real about our struggles and where we're at. I believe that when we choose to live authentically, we are letting go of the expectation to be perfect and we're allowing God's grace and mercy to lead the way. It plays a huge part in allowing our hearts to be free in Christ.

This little book is full of truths that have molded me into who I am today and who I am still learning to be. You're going to read about anxiety, grief, mistakes, abandonment, valleys, hardships, and heartache. But you're also going to read about restoration and how God is chasing after you, how He is holding your hand through every hard day and every easy day. And mostly you're going to read about how Jesus sets our hearts free.

He calls Me His own

It's Complicated

Out of nowhere an unwanted thought rudely crept in my mind: *You have so much baggage and you are so complicated.* This single thought sent my mind spiraling down a painful path—a path that reminded me of my parents' divorce, the massive mistakes I've made in my marriage, image issues, the broken relationship with my dad, and anxiety. The underlying lie that continued to creep in was, *Why am I so complicated?*

Then, a worship song just so happened to come on the radio, reminding me of how God actually sees me. He loves me. He holds me. He calls me His own. The song reminded me that, *Yes, I am complicated, but aren't we all?* Most days, I'm a mess. I can't shy away from who I am and where I've been. But at the end of the day, I don't really want to. There is so much freedom in allowing myself to be who I really am.

Couldn't we all benefit from embracing our messes? When the lies set in, remember to cling to His truths. If you're like me, you might be complicated, messy, and anxious, but God made us strong, loved, held, and His.

He goes to Battle for us

Turn Your Eyes

There are a lot of moments throughout our days that can easily get the best of us—little moments like hurt feelings from a friend or a disobedient child and big moments like heartache, broken relationships, or losing a loved one. These moments leave us feeling out of control and can easily send us spinning into a place of unknowns.

What I do know, though, is that God picks up our brokenness and puts us back together. And then He goes to battle for us and defends our hearts. It's so much better when we choose His way. Because, honestly, we can't make it on our own. So when the weight of the world is on our shoulders, we can turn our eyes away from darkness and toward the Light and the Hope. There is always, always hope when we're letting Him lead.

YOUR STORY WILL NOT BE WASTED.

He Will Do It Again

We have to keep going. Life can feel very heavy some days. Listen up, though: We can't lose hope. Think about the times that you've seen God's faithfulness in your life—His goodness, His mercy, and His restoration. During those days when you don't understand where He is or what He's doing, remember to trust God—remember that He is going to get you through this because He has done it before. Believe that He will do it again. Our stories will not be wasted—we will see God's glory in them someday soon. We must choose to hope even when we don't feel like it.

YOU'RE FREE

Rest in Hope

It's easy to crawl into bed at night and start dwelling on failures. Maybe you yelled at your kids, didn't study for a test hard enough, gossiped about a friend, or put yourself first more than you should have. Life is hard and sometimes our failures overtake us. Yet every night as we crawl into bed and think through our choices of the day, God is there gently reminding us, "You're forgiven." Every single night, He's saying, "You're free." On the hardest nights, when we're feeling alone and weighed down by the hardships of the day, He's holding us close saying, "You've got this. I'm with you. I'm not leaving you." He loves us and meets us right where we're at. He is gracious and patient. He sets our hearts and our minds free and then offers us a clean slate every single morning. Rest in that and hope in that. He is so good to us.

YOUR
MiSTakeS
do Not
DeFiNe
YOU.

Walk in Freedom

God didn't intend for us to wear scarlet letters revealing the mistakes we've made. He didn't send His Son to die for us so that we would continually dwell on our pasts and the choices we've made that have led to consequences. His gospel sets us free. We have a choice: We can walk around with our heads down because we're too scared to face the judgment of others, or we can hold our heads up high and walk with the freedom of Christ that He paid so much to give to us. We cannot let our sins hold us at ransom. He paid the whole bill, did the unthinkable, gave His own life so that we would be forgiven and set free. We can walk in that. We can be free in that. Our mistakes do not define us. The gospel and the freedom it provides do.

He calls you
Beautiful

You Are Made New

Whatever shame you're holding on to today, lay it at our Savior's feet. Whatever is weighing you down, let go of it. You are not bound to that shame, you are bound to Christ. In the moments when we're holding on to the things that tie us down, Jesus is gently whispering, "Hey, rest in Me. I have made you new." He loves us in spite of our sin, our struggles, our shame. He doesn't see us any differently; He doesn't think of us any less. We're accepted in Him and loved by Him, and Song of Solomon 4:7 says that He calls us beautiful. *Beautiful!*

Regardless of whatever weight is holding you down, you have a God who calls you beautiful and lavishes grace and mercy on you every single second of the day. Do not let your shame control who you are. Be free in who Christ made you to be and let His mercy wash over you when you're stuck in the hard places. He has made you new.

HE WILL CARRY US THROUGH

An Ending Place

Through. That's the word I cling to when I read Psalm 136:16: "To him who led his people *through* the wilderness, for his steadfast love endures forever." When I think of a wilderness, I think of a wild and uninhabited place, a neglected or abandoned area. That is oftentimes what it feels like when we go through periods of life that we don't understand. It can feel lonely, confusing, and like we are trapped in a place with no way out. And it can even feel like God has left us there to fend for ourselves.

Here's the deal, though: God's not going to lead us into a place and leave us. He will carry us *through.* And the word *through* means that there is another side—an ending place. This is where I find my comfort. The same God who will lead you in the wilderness will lead you out. If you are in the middle of a hard place, you will get *through* it. He is our deliverer and you can rest in His steadfast love.

CHOOSE to

WHEN YOU

Hope even don't feel like it.

LAY IT ALL DOWN

24

Wave the White Flag

What is holding you captive right now? What is weighing you down?

Is it discontentment in your circumstances? Lay it down.

Is it pride or anger? Lay it down.

Is it guilt or shame? Lay it all down.

We are all facing battles within us that hold our hearts and our minds captive. They weigh us down and bind us up and make us feel like we are at war with our struggles. There is such good news, though. Lay those battles down at the feet of Jesus and wave the white flag of surrender because Luke 4:18 says that He came to set the captives free. He proclaims liberty over you!—so that you can proclaim victory over your heaviness, over your guilt, over your shame. Jesus has fought the battle for you and has won. Let those truths cover your heart and your mind and allow the heaviness to subside. Walk in freedom!

walk
boldly
and
bravely

Believe

There's a story in Mark 5 about a very sick and dying little girl. Her dad knew Jesus was coming into town so he ran to find Him and begged Him to come heal his daughter. By the time they got back to the house, the little girl had died and everyone hopelessly said that it was too late. But Jesus said to the family, "Do not fear, only believe." And He walked over to the girl, took her hand, and said, "Little girl, I say to you, arise." She immediately got up and walked around and everyone stared in amazement.

Listen, whatever you are going through today that is causing you worry and anxiety, stop being so afraid and just believe. Believe that Jesus has your best interests in His hands, that He will heal your brokenness and your wounds. Believe that He will call you to rise up, that He will call you to walk in His freedom, just like He did with the little girl in Mark 5. Walk boldly and bravely in that freedom. Turn your eyes to Jesus and stand in amazement of the One who has healed you and set you free.

god's Love is so much better than life

Better than Life

I love how David cries out to the Lord in Psalm 63:3 when he says, "Because your steadfast love is better than life, my lips will praise you." Can you imagine it? David is lonely, sitting in a dry, desert wilderness with no water. He is longing to see the Lord and to feel His presence, and he's tired of being patient. But when I read Psalm 63:3, I hear his faith in the Lord. David remembers how God's love is so much better than even life itself, and because of that, he will choose to continue to praise Him—even when he doesn't feel the Lord, even when he can't see what He's doing.

I think about this a lot when I feel like I'm in my own dry and weary desert, when I'm tired of crying out to the Lord and not getting any answers. But then when I think about all He has done and all He will continue to do, when I think about how His love is so much better than life, I choose to continue to praise Him. His steadfast love is better than life!

Feel the freedom

Feel the Freedom

People can be disappointing sometimes. We make mistakes, we hurt feelings, we don't meet expectations—realistic and unrealistic. We are human, and we don't measure up sometimes to what is wanted or needed from us. But holding on to those disappointments can feel so heavy and add so much weight in our day-to-day lives. When we let go of a hurt that caused great disappointment in someone, we are free from the weight and the bitterness we are harboring in our hearts. Let someone off the hook today and allow yourself to feel the freedom that overwhelms your heart because you did so.

take heart daughter

He Sets Us Free

There's a story in Matthew 9 about a woman who had been bleeding for twelve years—twelve years! That is 4,383 days! This woman probably spent money on doctors who gave her no answers. She was considered unclean and held her head down in shame—for twelve years! Until one day. The day she saw Jesus walking by. And in her suffering, she said, "If I only touch his garment, I will be made well" (9:21). So she did. She touched His cloak. That faith was all she needed for Jesus to turn and tell her, "Take heart, daughter; your faith has made you well" (9:22).

Imagine hearing those words! To be able to turn and walk away *free* from what made her so unclean. I am sure there were days when she was absolutely miserable. There were *days* when she just didn't feel like waiting anymore. And yet, she just walked right up and touched His cloak with boldness and confidence. Maybe it's time for us to walk up and touch His cloak. Let's kiss doubt goodbye and allow Jesus to heal our restless hearts. Let's know that He sets us *free* with one gentle turn of His head.

He uses the tough times to teach us the most.

Growing Stronger

A few years ago, I decided to try running. (You should know that I've never enjoyed running, and I have no idea why I wanted to try it.) At first, I could only run for a few minutes before I was stopped by a painful burning feeling in my legs. Over time, though, I learned that it was this burning feeling that was actually making me stronger. In fact, I found myself pushing my body harder so I would always feel the burn. If I wasn't feeling it, I wasn't working hard enough.

I think our relationship with the Lord is a lot like learning how to run. He oftentimes uses the tough times to teach us the most. In those moments, I wish it wouldn't hurt as much as it does. But then I come out stronger, I work harder, and I let Him push me further.

There have been heart-wrenching days. Suffocating days. Broken-hearted days. Those days make me ready for the next time so that I can go even farther. Without those seasons that God's given me, I'd still be running one lap and walking the rest, feeling no burn, and staying exactly the same.

TODAY HAS NEW grace

Power and Victory

Yesterday was a day full of disappointments, discouragements, mistakes, and failures. I woke up this morning with a heavy heart—my eyes puffy from crying so many tears the night before. I knew I had a choice. I could hang on to all of it and bring it into today, or I could let it go and receive all the new mercies God had intended for me. Today is new. Today has new grace. Today I can choose to not let my enemies claim anything over me. I am not defined by my bad day yesterday. I am loved. I have power and victory through the Holy Spirit to fight off all the convincing lies of the enemy. I can lay it all down at the foot of the cross and walk in freedom today. That's the best news, for me and for you.

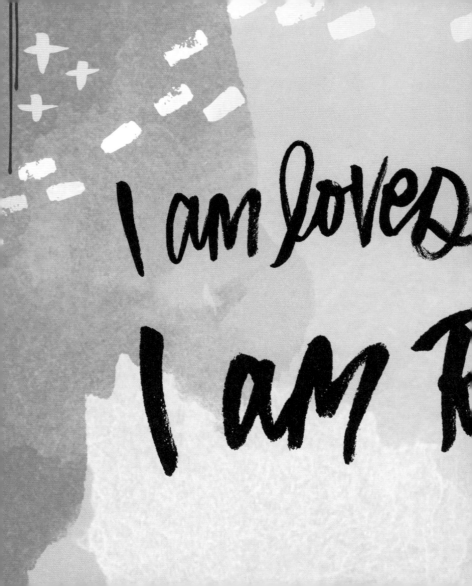

am forgiven.

estored.

Feel His
Mercy +
grace wash
over you.

Find Your Sunset

I find God in sunsets. There is a secret spot in my little town, and when I'm having a hard day, I sneak away to my spot for a little bit to regroup and to find beauty in my day. I sit quietly. Sometimes crying, sometimes just watching. I may not always hear His voice, but I feel really close to Him in those few moments. I love watching the sky change colors, especially when pink clouds appear overhead. In those moments, I allow His mercies to cover me. I allow His grace to wash over me. It becomes all I need.

Finding those moments during the day helps me feel connected and close to the Lord in ways that draw me in to His freedom—in ways that release me from whatever is holding me back. What draws you in? What helps you feel His mercy and grace wash over you? Maybe it's driving with the windows down, maybe it's a quiet walk alone, maybe it's having a cup of coffee in your favorite chair. Whatever it may be, allow those moments to bring you the freedom only He can provide.

He is
Always
Right
There.

Run into His Arms

Shame is such a sneaky little thing. You work so hard to get rid of it and then it just creeps up on you when you least expect it. I've made some large mistakes, and as much as I have experienced God's grace and redemption in such a real way, something can trigger a memory and the shame floods in like a tidal wave. It's in those moments that I have to constantly remind myself that I am a child of the King. I am loved, I am forgiven, I am restored.

So, in the moments when the shame wants to take over, we need to hold our heads up high and be confident in the fact that we have a God who loves us at our worst moments and at our best. He cancels out the shame with His grace. He wants to rid our hearts and our minds of it and replace it with His new mercies every single morning. So when the guilt of our past starts to overwhelm our minds, let's turn away from it and run into God's open arms. He is always right there.

God's Peace FLOODS OUR Hearts

Flooded with Peace

Grief. It comes in so many different forms. The loss of a loved one, the loss of a dream, the loss of what you thought life would be. There are so many things that are hard to understand. Grief can trap you and suffocate you. It can make you feel like you're walking around with bricks as shoes because it just feels so heavy and your heart and body feel so burdened.

Grief gets easier with time and can start to feel bearable. But it never leaves. It can be tricky to navigate because you might have a moment that feels a little cloudy and before you know it, a storm has blown in and you're lost in the heartache of losing something or someone. That is where God's peace comes in and floods our hearts. It doesn't take away the pain, but it washes over us and covers us and that becomes all we need. God's peace surpasses our understanding, and He is holding your hand and walking with you through every painful moment and every joyful moment. Let your heart rest in that.

god fills all the voids

He Is Not Going Anywhere

For three years, I've been walking through the pain of abandonment. An unexpected broken relationship left a very weird and painful hole that I am still getting used to. It has been one of the hardest things I have ever gone through. Here's the deal, though. I've experienced God in a different way. I've talked to Him when I didn't know how to talk about this and I've cried to Him when I wasn't ready to cry to anyone else. He has truly filled voids.

God has reminded me over and over that He is not abandoning me. He is staying. He is not going anywhere. When the darkness closes in on me, He's there to reassure me. And you know...whatever you're dealing with today—God is staying with you too. He will not leave you either. This truth has been my saving grace—it has helped me get through every painful day and it can help you get through yours too. He promises in Deuteronomy 31:6 to never leave us. So hold on to hope! God is staying, holding our hands, walking with us in the dark until we feel safe again.

WHO I AM is ENOUGH

Beautiful

The world does a fantastic job of telling us who we are supposed to be. We need to be successful with money, a fancy car, and a dream home. We need to be beautiful with perfect cheekbone structures and full lips. Our clothes need to be styled with the most up-to-date trends, and our homes need to be decorated with whatever is popular on Instagram these days. It can be really, really draining to try to keep up.

I've learned that I don't have to be anyone except who God created me to be. And who I am is enough. I don't need to compare my success to anyone else's. He has created me capable, strong, and brave. I don't need to compare my outward appearance to anyone else's, He has created me beautiful in His eyes. When I stop looking to the world for approval in my day-to-day life and start looking for approval in the eyes of my Creator, I realize I am exactly who I should be. It gives me freedom to be myself and to be true to who I am as a woman following hard after Christ.

He will
NEVER
STOP
loving
us...

God Rescues

During one of the worst years of my life, nighttime was very daunting. The darkness would close in on me in a very real way. Anxiety would make itself known, and I would spend hours lying in uncertainty, hoping for the morning.

I read one day in Exodus 14 about the battle between the Israelites and the Egyptians. The Israelites were desperate to be free from their enemies, and the Lord continually provided a way. But not without hardship. At one point the Israelites were scared to death of the next step, and they were constantly crying out to the Lord until He said, "I am fighting for you. You just need to be silent."

From then on, God rescued them every time the Egyptians came close. He even parted the Red Sea for them. God went before them. And He goes before us. He hears our cries in the darkest of dark nights and rescues us. He will never stop fighting for us, He will never stop saving us from the battles we are facing. Let your heart rest in that. Let His peace calm you, and be still and silent before Him. He is fighting for you.

LET GOD CALM YOUR SEAS.

Release

Sometimes on a busy day or a hard day or a day that seems entirely impossible from start to finish, I like to close my eyes and imagine myself on a drive through back roads with the windows down. I imagine the sun's rays shining through the trees as the fresh air blows through my hair and my outstretched hand. And I can almost picture God saying, "Let Me be the One who sustains you right here, in this place where you are. Let it be Me who calls your name and calms your heart with My voice. Let it be Me who calms your seas and stops your storms. Let it be Me who calms you with My peace that is beyond your understanding." Once I've let that gentle voice run through my mind and through my heart, whatever grip I've had on the hardship of the day starts to loosen, and I start to experience the freedom of letting go of the hard places.

Look for ways to hear God's gentle voice throughout the day and allow Him to sustain your heart. He delights in it.

live in exciTes
at what He
Throug

amazement
s going to do
you.

He will
make your
Heart
come Alive
again

Embrace Hope

There's a story in John 11 about a man named Lazarus. Lazarus was a close friend of Jesus who became very sick. Lazarus's sisters reached out to Jesus to tell Him Lazarus was about to die, and Jesus assured them that the sickness would not result in death—which was strange, because by the time Jesus got to Lazarus, he had already died. Jesus knew He was going to raise him from the dead, but He still chose to weep and mourn over the loss of His friend before He did. He embraced the pain and felt what Lazarus's sisters and family felt and comforted them. And then Jesus asked them to trust Him, to trust that He would raise their brother from the dead. And He did. He called Lazarus to wake up, and Lazarus woke up.

When you are heartbroken, remember that Jesus felt that same pain. He knows what it's like to experience deep sorrow. Embracing the pain is not showing a lack of trust in the Lord. Feel your emotions and have hope in the Lord. Trust that He will make your heart come alive again.

WE ARE SAFE IN GOD'S HANDS.

You're Safe

The word *reed* is defined as a weak or impressionable person. I know because I read Isaiah 42:3 and had to look it up. The verse says, "A bruised reed he will not break." That verse and definition comforted me because in a lot of ways, I am a weak person. I am encouraged by the fact that I am safe in God's hands.

No matter the burden you're carrying, you are not alone in carrying it. Whether it be addiction, depression, failed dreams, financial stress, anxiety, divorce...whatever it may be, you have a Savior who does not think it is a burden. He knows your heart. He sees inside to the depths of your soul. He loves you in a real way. He gives grace to you in a big way. He will not break you; you are safe in His hands. He draws near to the brokenhearted and binds up their wounds. Rest and be free in the fact that you are safe and taken care of in the hands of Christ.

HE WILL TURN TEARS INTO LAUGHTER

Tears to Laughter

Psalm 56:8 says, "You have kept count of my tossings; put my tears in your bottle." Isn't it so encouraging to know that we belong to a God who keeps track of every restless night? He keeps track of every tear cried. He is tenderhearted toward us and full of compassion. He cares about those restless nights and those countless tears so much more than we can even comprehend. The good news is that He is so ready to turn that restlessness into peace. He is so ready to turn those tears into laughter. He is so ready to turn our captivity into freedom. He will turn our mourning into dancing. We have a God who loves us that much!

HOLD ONTO HOPE

Lighthearted Hope

It gets better. I wish I could tell you the exact formula for how you're going to get through this, but all I know is that one of these mornings you're going to wake up and your heart is going to feel lighter and your feet are going to want to dance. It's a gradual process, and then all of a sudden you realize He's healed your heavy heart and set it free. Jesus heals us like no one and nothing else can or will. He picks up all of our messy, broken pieces and puts them back together in such a fresh and new way. So wherever you are in this moment right now, hold onto hope. You won't always be there. God has a plan to do something so much bigger with your heart and with your life.

Be True to
WHO YOU ARe
iN CHRiST

You Be You

Everywhere we turn, our culture is saying, "Be yourself." I get it, I really do. I think it is one of the best things you can do for yourself to be true to who you are. What I think we are missing is what Jesus is saying to us, which is, "Find yourself in Me." Be true to who you are, but be true to who you are *in Christ*. You were created with a purpose. You were created with a calling for your life. When you pursue the Lord with all your heart, your soul, and your mind, that calling and purpose become more and more clear and transform you into who He wants you to be. The more you seek His face, the more you discover how to be true to who God intended you to become. There is so much freedom in that. There is so much freedom in surrendering who our culture is telling you to be and choosing to be who you are in Jesus.

THERE is
HOPE
in THE
WAITING

Embrace the Wait

I know how hard it is to wait. To wait for one chapter of your life to end and a new one to begin, to wait for a fresh season. Waiting can be exhausting, and patience can grow thin. Listen, don't waste this in-between time. As you are waiting for what's next, whatever it may be, learn to enjoy today. Maybe you're waiting for answers, maybe you're waiting for healing, maybe you're waiting for shame to go away or heartache to diminish. God is here with you today just as much as He will be here with you tomorrow. So don't waste today. Embrace it. Find beauty in it. There is wonderful joy ahead (I Peter 1:6), but trust in the Lord that He will make something beautiful out of today. There is hope in the waiting. Come alive in that hope.

LIGHT
ALWAYS
WINS
OVER
DARK

The Light Always Wins

You might be living in such darkness right now that you are afraid your heart is incapable of ever knowing the light again. You might be deep in sin, overwhelmed with shame, embarrassed of bad choices, or overcome with guilt. I get it. I really do. I want you to know something. There is no way for darkness to win over light. In a room darker than midnight, the smallest flicker of a match will light up the whole place. You do not need to dwell in this place, in this darkness. There may be a war going on inside of you, but you have a God who will fight that battle for you on the darkest night (Exodus 14:14, Matthew 4:16).

YOUR HEART
PeTTLe, PeACe
you, aNd

WILL

WILL WASH OVER

THE RUN WILL

START SHINING

again.

god is
PREPARING
you foR
SOMETHING
AMAZING

He Has Great Plans for You

God never said following Him would be easy. In fact, in a lot of ways, it is one of the hardest things you will ever choose to do. Don't get me wrong. Your life is going to be so full and rich and beautiful. But there will be hard days. Really hard ones. If you're feeling weary right now, be encouraged. God is preparing you for something amazing. He sees you, He knows your heart, and He's going to use you. Stay the course. Don't give up, even on the hardest days. He's not looking for people who have it all together, who speak eloquently, who show strength at all times. He's just looking for people who follow hard after Him—who surrender their messy lives and their weary hearts in order to ultimately bring Him glory. Live in excited amazement at what He is going to do through you.

He Sees Your
Beautiful
Heart.

God Thinks You're Beautiful

If you've ever made a terrible mistake and you're worried about what people think of you, I understand. I've been there. I know what it's like to walk around with my head down for months because I'm scared to look up for fear of what I'll see in people's eyes when they look at me. I want you to know something: God is never looking at you with disgust. He's not looking at you like you're a failure or a mess-up. He's not looking at you with anything other than forgiveness. He's looking at you with tender grace and new mercies. He's turning toward you, lifting your head, and transforming you.

GOD is
CHASING
AFTER YOU.

He Is Chasing after You

You might have woken up this morning with the mistakes of yesterday weighing on your shoulders so greatly that you didn't feel like getting out of bed. They could be the worst mistakes you've ever made or the repetitive kind that you make every day. Either way, they're still making it hard for you to face the day. You don't know where to turn, who to call, how to make it today. The shame feels suffocating and the guilt is trapping you. Every step feels like you're walking on sinking sand.

I have excellent news: There is a loving God who is chasing after you with His beauty and His love. He is waiting for you with arms that are open, ready for you to run in. He is relentlessly pursuing you and is calling for you to come back to Him. I know you feel lost right now, but He will not give up on searching for His children until they are back in His arms. There is freedom there and you may not feel like you deserve it, but that is what grace is. He's waiting for you, He's chasing hard after you, and He's not giving up on you.

you are
Radically
loveD
by god.

You Are Radically Loved

At your very worst moment, Jesus looks at you and whispers, "Come here. I'm waiting for you." At the moment that you feel like your life is falling apart, Jesus is already putting it back together. You feel alone and broken, but He is right there holding you. You might feel heavy and bound to something, but He is lightening your load as we speak. He's breaking the chains and freeing up your soul. Jesus is not looking at you with disappointment or frustration, He's looking at you and saying, "You're My child, and I love you." You might feel like you don't measure up to what Jesus is looking for, but He's standing in front of you saying, "It's you that I want. Run to Me."

You are radically loved by God. He is delighted with you and crazy about you, and He wants you to find freedom in Him. Doesn't it feel amazing to be loved like that?

Feel god's STReNGTH rising up wiTHiN.

You're Getting Stronger

This waiting you're doing right now might be one of the hardest things you have ever had to do. You're waiting for open doors and there's uncertainty. Your heart gets anxious and it becomes hard to be still and patient. In these moments, God is strengthening you and preparing you for what He's going to do in your life. You're getting stronger by the minute, and pretty soon you're going to start to feel God's peace calming you. Your waiting period might not be over and you might not have all the answers you need yet, but by the grace of God, you're going to learn how to hang in there. You're going to learn that pretty soon everything is going to be okay and you're going to learn that God was calming your anxious heart all along. So take a deep breath and feel God's strength start rising up within you and His stillness wash over your mind and your heart.

LET YOUR feet
dance in His
FREEDOM.

Walk in the Light

There are some days that your heart feels restless and your soul feels weary. Everything feels heavy and yet somehow, you've got to find the strength to walk out the door. You're tired. Tired of doing what is right and tired of staying strong. Listen, do not be discouraged. Do not give up. Galatians 6:9 says that pretty soon you're going to reap a harvest of blessing.

You may feel like the days are dark right now, but God is calling you to come out from that darkness and walk into His light. He wants you to dance in it, to be free in it, to let that Light make you feel alive again. Let your restless heart find strength and your weary soul find courage in the One Who created you to walk in His light. Let your feet dance in that freedom.

god bReaks
eveRy
single
CHAIN

A Beautiful Picture

What I love about the gospel is that we are standing before God with every single flaw and mistake exposed, and instead of judgment and anger He's handing us forgiveness, no questions asked. When you stand back and think about it—*really* think about it—it is a beautiful example of freedom. Because as you're standing there broken and bound, He's breaking every single chain and drawing you closer to Him. He's saying, "I know you have sinned greatly against Me, but there is grace right here in this place."

It's impossible to fully understand it, but this is the gospel. We deserve none of it and yet He's handing this freedom over to us with such tenderness, such healing, such mercy flooding into our souls. And all we can do is embrace it and be free. All we have to offer God in return is our flawed selves living our lives surrendered to Him. It is a beautiful picture of freedom and grace, and it is the gospel.

Jesus draws

the broken

birds up

near to
arted and
ur wounds.

HiS VoiCe CaLMS THE STorMS.

God Calms the Storms

I love the story in Matthew 8 when Jesus is with His disciples on a boat and a violent storm comes out of nowhere. The disciples were so afraid and Jesus said, "Why are you afraid?" And then He told the wind to be silent and the sea to quiet down. The disciples were shocked at the power of Jesus! His voice silenced the wind and waves.

We all go through storms in our lives. Some are small, but others hit us just as violently as the one in Matthew 8. God is not going to bring you into a storm alone, though. He is going before you, standing beside you, surrounding you with protection. You might feel like your ship is going down, but with His voice, God is in control. He's saying, "My child, why are you so fearful? Just trust Me." And before you know it, those rocky waters and those rapid winds will calm and you'll be on the other side of the storm. Your heart will settle, peace will wash over you, and the sun will start shining again. His voice calms the storms. Let it calm your soul.

Jesus Loves you & Calls you His Child.

Simply Be

Your past is not what defines you, and neither is your present. The mountain you're facing or the winding road you're walking right now...those don't define you either. The heartache you're bearing, the loss you're grieving, the guilt you're holding onto, the tasks on your to-do list...none of these things define you. You are defined by your worth in Christ. By the way He loves you and calls you His child. That is where you can find your identity—that is where you can find the truth. All other things pulling you in opposite directions are not what determine the outcome of your day, your month, your year. You are a child loved by Jesus, who calls you worthy, who lavishes His grace on you and lifts your daily burdens. Find your worth there. Let that define who you are and who you're called to be.

god is Not
LeaViNg
nour SiDe

Rest in the Confusion

Life might feel confusing right now, but be assured that it is not confusing for God. Things might not feel very smooth at the moment, and maybe you're doubting what He's up to. But He has such a beautiful plan for this season, and He has woven His grace so intricately through it. You might not be able to understand Him right now or see Him, but He is always there. He gently wakes you up in the morning with the reminder that it is a fresh day and new mercies are following you everywhere you go. He's holding your hand through every good moment and every hard moment of this day and He's not leaving your side. He's showing Himself to you in ways you cannot understand quite yet, but as He continues to reveal His plan to you, you will begin to see Him. He is changing you, making you new, strengthening you in this confusion. He wants you to find rest and peace in Him.

walk in god's
FREEDOM

Surrender

I know what it feels like to be caught making the worst mistake of your life. To be embarrassed and humiliated by your sin, devastated by your own choices, wondering how you found yourself in this web of darkness and lies. You don't know how you're going to get up in the morning and face the day, face people you've hurt, face the Lord. I understand. I've been there. What I want you to know is this: the same God who created the universe, the God who put the stars into their places, the God who breathed life into you is now saying, "Find Me in your brokenness."

When we choose to allow the devastation of our sin and our choices to bring us to our knees, to break our hearts, to overwhelm us with grief and sorrow, it is in those moments that God is saying, "You are set free because of Jesus's blood. You are forgiven." Allow that brokenness to turn into surrendering and walk in God's freedom and redemption. He has set your heart free!

His gospel is Peace

Hold On Tight

Maybe you're in a season where you feel like you can't quite catch your breath, when some days feel like you'll never stop learning the same lesson. Maybe you're in a season where you're having really, really great days and then some days feel longer than they've ever been. You're crying big, huge, exhausted tears one minute, and the next minute you're laughing until you can't stop and joy is seeping out of every corner.

Some days you feel the weight of the world on you, and some days you feel lightness in every step. One thing never changes though: His gospel is peace. On the best day and on the worst day, it floods your heart with steadfast joy, truth, and grace. It brings freedom and light to every season you're in. Hold on tight to it and let it transform your life.

WE HAVE THE
POWER OF
JESUS IN US

Power over Lies

My mind is often where I face the biggest battles. I wake up every morning and have to fight the lies and doubts constantly being fed to me. Oftentimes, I let those lies win and I believe them. I believe that I'm not good enough, that I'm not capable enough, that my mistakes of yesterday were carried into today, that my past is still part of my present. I know I'm not the only one. I know we all face lies that the enemy desperately wants us to believe over the truth.

Listen, these mind battles can create character in us. We have the power of Christ in our hearts to claim victory over them! We need to put on our armor, let the Truth of Jesus flood our minds, and take charge of this war. Satan cannot win this, the enemy cannot overcome this. We have the power of Jesus in us to proclaim freedom over these lies and to not allow the enemy to have authority over us.

Today, let Christ take over because the gospel has already won. Claim victory over the lies and believe the Truth that is in front of you.

live with
Reckless
ABANDON

Life to the Fullest

Today is a new day, and you have one chance to live it. God has given you this day, and you can choose if you want to waste it or live it fully. You might have woken up weary and discouraged. You can stay there or you can let God give you rest. You can swim in uncertainty today or you can let God be your confidence. Maybe you're feeling insecure; you can choose to let God sustain you. Today you can choose to be held captive or you can choose to be set free. But you only have one chance to live today. Live it with your hands held high, surrendered in worship to the Lord. Live it with grace and freedom. Because once tomorrow comes, today will be gone, and your chance to leave behind something fully lived will be over. You have been given today! Today you are alive! Live it well.

He caRRies the fiRe. He acRoss AtlaK

you across
guides you
waters.

God is drawing near to you.

God Will Never Leave You

It's okay to not be okay. It's okay to feel like you don't have the strength to do this. I understand and I've been there. Everything feels like it's falling apart and you feel like giving up. It can be hard to understand what God's doing or trust in His plan.

There are going to be days when you feel like you are the strongest you've ever been, and there are going to be days when you're just trying to put one foot in front of the other. That's okay. When it's hard to feel God's presence, He is just as close. He is drawing near to you saying, "I know every single intricate piece of your life. I made you and I know the plans I have for you. Today you might feel weak, but I am making you strong. You might feel torn into pieces, but I am making you new again. You might not feel very brave today, but your light is still shining. I will hold you, I will be beside you, I will not leave you. Rest in Me."

His hope and His power will shine through.

He Turns Dark to Light

In Isaiah 61, God tells us He will make beauty out of our ashes. It started with the Israelites. When a loved one would die or during a period of intense trials and tragedy, they would cover themselves with ashes to show their sorrow or repentance. It was an act of mourning. When God told them He was going to turn their ashes into beauty, what He was saying was He was going to take their sorrows and trials and turn them into something beautiful. God understands our darkness and our grief and our brokenness, but He is ready to set us free from them. Those ashes don't cover us forever. They will wash away, and His hope and His power will shine through.

You might feel like you're still covered with the ashes of your grief and your trials. It might not make any sense right now. But God is healing you, redeeming you, restoring you, and turning the darkness and the ugliness into something so beautiful, you won't even believe it. Hold on to that hope.

God's Perfect grace is Never changing.

God's Perfect Grace

There is purpose in this trial you are walking through. It might be the hardest thing you've ever been through, but I believe you are going to look back and see how much stronger God made you become. Your life feels messy and imperfect right now, but God's perfect grace is never changing and is carrying you through. Your heart is still free even in the midst of this aching. You are still able to be at perfect peace with the Lord even in the midst of this turmoil. You are still brave even if you feel weak. You don't know what is around the bend, but God is doing something incredible in you through this process. You are learning to trust in the Lord—even when you can't see the end of the road. There is going to be wonderful, incredible joy before you know it.

He carries you across the fire

God Carries You

The thing about anxiety: it hits you at the weirdest moments. It comes and goes as it pleases. It humiliates you, leaves you lonely and drained. It sends you to a dark place and makes it feel as if a war is taking place inside you.

The thing about Jesus though: He never leaves your side. He's always there, always whispering in your ear, "Hey, I'm here. And you're going to be just fine." He carries you across the fire. He breathes mercy into you with every breath. He overcomes it all. Everything. Every ounce of anxiousness that creeps into your mind, your heart, your most tender places—He has already overcome it. He's with you when you're curled in a ball crying huge tears into your pillow. He's with you when you are smiling and pretending that everything is perfectly fine but your insides are screaming. He never leaves your side.

If you're just trying to survive every day, let me reassure you—I understand. You are not alone. You are going to be okay. He is with you, and He is carrying you. You are stronger than you think, braver than you know, and you are going to be okay.

FLOWERS DON'T GROW IN SUNSHINE ONLY.

Flowers Need Rain

When storms are over, everything smells like new life. Colors are more vibrant, birds are singing louder, skies look bluer, and the grass is a brighter shade of green. Isn't that how life is? The storms come and there are days when you don't know if you're going to survive. You're worried and tired, and the list of unknowns seems impossible. You know the only way you're going to get through this is by trusting the Lord because you have no clue how to make it without Him.

And then one day the heavens open up and these huge rays of sunshine come breaking through the clouds, the kind of rays that stop you in your tracks and take your breath away. And everything in you breathes new life again. Your storm is over and now you see the growth. Flowers don't grow in sunshine only. They need rain. We don't grow in carefree times only. We need trials to teach us. When those storms are over, though, that is when we can jump in the puddles and dance in His freedom.

LET GOD'S PRESENCE OVERWHELM YOU.

Let His Peace Wash over You

It is so easy to praise the Lord when things are going great and life feels good. It's easy to worship and to be in adoration when we're happy and carefree—to sing hallelujahs and to raise our hands with no holding back. But then when life gets hard and when fear creeps in and when we just don't understand God's plan, those hallelujahs don't come as easy.

Listen, do not let the darkness take away those praises. Sing them louder. Raise those hands as high up to the sky as you can raise them. Let those tears fall with no shame. Let your voice shake with no worries. Let God's presence overwhelm you, let His peace wash over you, and let it calm your fears. Run into His arms with nothing holding you back, knowing He is going to catch you. His cross made a way for the freedom in your heart—do not let anything take that away. Keep singing your praises, sing them loudly, and do not lose heart. He is right there with you.

WALK IN HIS LIGHT.

He Calls You His Child

If you're feeling broken right now, maybe the hurt you're experiencing feels suffocating. You're walking with an ache in your heart and you don't know how to shake it. Or maybe the sin you're living in is overwhelming you with darkness. You feel trapped with no way out. I want you to know that Jesus has saved you. With His power, He can break you away from your sin, and with His power He can heal your brokenness.

He rescues us, He opens our hearts, and He covers the lies with the power of His truth. He calls us His children. He calls us righteous. And He calls us to follow Him. It is time to let go of whatever is holding you back and choose to walk in His light. He made you, He saves you, and He frees you. And most of all, He loves you. He deeply, deeply loves you.

THERE'S ONLY

to WHO TRULY

intricate

one I can turn

Knows every

part of my

Heart.

His ways are Higher than our own.

Walk in Confidence

We were made with a purpose. Jeremiah 29 says He has our lives all planned out. It says He's going to take care of us and not abandon us.

So when life feels confusing, messy, chaotic, or frustrating, we need to remember that none of this is a surprise to God. When things aren't going at all how we thought they would or how we planned, God is not thrown off by the chaos. He's in complete control and has full knowledge of the road ahead. He says, "You will call upon me and come and pray to me, and I will hear you. You will seek me and find me, when you seek me with all your heart" (Jeremiah 29:12–13). We need to relinquish control of what we are holding onto for our lives and walk in confidence that God has His purpose and plan for our lives, and His ways are so much higher and better than our own.

THINK ABOUT LOVELY THINGS.

Think Happy Thoughts

When your mind is flooded with lies, dig deep in your heart and find the things you know to be true. Think about those things instead. When you're being tempted by sin and by shame and you don't know how to turn away, think about what is honorable to the Lord. When you're focused on things that are evil and wicked, set your heart on what is just. If your thoughts have turned to things corrupt or dishonest, purify your mind. Think about things that bring God glory instead of shame. Think about lovely things—things that bring beauty to your day.

When your mind is dwelling on anything false, impure, unjust, and disgraceful, fight for freedom and for joy with all your might and think about everything worthy of praise. It requires hard work, but it will be so rewarding when your mind is set free from lies and dwells on truth instead.

He will Meet every Need.

Be Still and Know

I love how Psalm 121:1–2 says, "I lift my eyes up to the hills. From where does my help come? My help comes from the LORD, who made heaven and earth." People are going to let us down, situations are going to let us down. Life might not be going exactly how we want it to be going. Whatever our situations are, our help comes from the Lord. Nothing else on this earth will satisfy our needs. The only place we will find our strength is from the Lord. He will meet every need we have and sustain us in the places we are. It's so very freeing to recognize this! He is where our help and our strength come from. We can be still and rest in Him!

god will guide you

Give It All to God

Have you ever been stuck in a dark valley, but you're in far too deep to admit it? So you ignore it, pretend it doesn't exist, or hide from it so you don't have to face it head-on? Maybe you just don't even know how deep in that valley you really are. Maybe it's sin, grief, or a broken relationship?

It's so easy to miss the signs that it's time to let go. We say, "It's really not that bad" or "I'll deal with it later." We ignore what we're holding on to and push it away, and we keep smiling like nothing is wrong. And because we do that, we never let these things reach the surface, and we miss the opportunity to hand them over to the Lord. Listen, I get how hard it is. It feels scary and we're afraid to let go because we're so attached. Sometimes we don't even realize how attached we really are. But we have a God who wants to help us. Cry out to Him, tell Him you cannot do this on your own, and He will not miss a beat. He will free you.

god wants
us to be
FREE.

Expectations vs. Reality

I have high expectations of myself. I like to have my ducks in a row, and I like to do a really good job on my responsibilities. When something happens that doesn't align with my hopes or my plans, it is really hard for me to let go of the disappointment I feel in myself. I get weighed down by the pressure of measuring up to what I'm expecting and having it all together.

What I've learned—and honestly am still learning—is that God just doesn't want that from us. He wants us to let go of those expectations we have put on ourselves, and He wants to carry the weight of them for us. His yoke is easy and His burden is light. He wants us to be free from thinking that we have to have it all together and be who we are—messy, imperfect people living for Him.

He dreams.
with us.

God Has Big Dreams for You

Life can be completely disappointing sometimes. We think, hope, pray it's going to go one way and instead it goes in a totally different direction. There are tears, confusion, and unanswered questions. And suddenly there's a lack of control because the future is out of our hands. This is where we have to let go. We have to let go of what we thought this season would look like, this year, this life. This is where trust comes in.

We have to surrender our dreams and our desires and trust in God's plan, even when it doesn't look like our own. We have to remember that God is just. He is not going to plan out a life for us that we can't handle. He loves us. He dreams with us. He is also trustworthy. Let go of the disappointments when the plans you desperately wanted don't work out, and trust that God has your best interests and your best dreams in mind.

LET god
HOLD YOU.

Release Your Grip

Being in a hard season for longer than you expected can be draining. You're tired, you're losing hope, you're losing steam. You've been praying for relief and answers and they're just not coming yet. You're holding on tight, but your grip is loosening a little more each day. Here's what I've learned: If you're stuck, God isn't finished teaching you here yet. There are still lessons for you to learn. He has big plans for you here, and you're going to understand them one day soon. He is going to keep giving you the exact amount of patience and strength that you need to make it through every single day. He's going to give you grace when you feel like giving up.

So let go of your control and let go of your grip and let God take over. Let Him hold on for you. And let your heart be free here. Let your heart be free to embrace His mercies and the lessons He is teaching you. Let God hold your hand and guide you to the other side.

THE Aame goa

in the wilde

will lead

tHAT · Led you

eNESS.

you out.

He wants us just the way we are.

Open Your Door

I made a mistake awhile back and it was a pretty big one. I let a lot of people down and it felt like my world was crumbling around me. I knew at that point that I had a choice. I could either let people in on the fact that my marriage isn't perfect, my parenting isn't perfect, my life isn't perfect—or I could try to pretend that it all is. I could quickly shove messes into closets when people announce they're dropping by to make it appear that my house is spotless clean all the time, or I could just leave the messes and allow friends to see the real deal. I decided to let people in on the truth and live authentically in Christ.

Most days, I have nothing figured out. I'm just trying to make it! I think when we let go of the need to appear like we have it all together, we give others the freedom to live authentically as well. The truth is that God has set us free from feeling the weight of the need to be perfect! He wants us just the way we are.

GOD LOVES, accepts, + sustains us.

He Already Approves of You

You know what is really hard for me sometimes? The fact that not everyone is going to like me. I'm not very good at accepting that reality. For my entire life I have always struggled with the approval of others—and when someone doesn't like me, support me, or accept me, it hurts. As I've gotten more confident in who God has made me to be, the need for approval from others isn't as important. There are going to be people who don't believe in me, who don't support me, who don't like the ways I do things. Those people are not who matter and neither is their acceptance. I have a God who loves me, who made me, who accepts me, who goes before me, and who sustains me. And He is the One who matters.

Once we let go of our need for approval from others around us, we are free to really embrace the acceptance we receive from the One who created us.

Let go. Surrender. Be Free.

Follow Him

When Jesus called the disciples to follow Him in Luke 9, He simply said, "Follow Me." He did not ask them to, and He didn't give them any further instructions on what that might look like. He just said, "Follow Me." Some responses weren't pretty. One disciple said, "I have to go bury my father first." Another disciple said, "I want to say goodbye to my friends and family first." Both times Jesus said, "No, I just want you to follow Me." He wanted them to let go of the things that were holding them back and the life they thought would be better and just follow Him.

I believe Jesus is still calling us to let go of whatever is hindering us, and to follow Him with everything we've got. We are holding on to what we think is a better life, but you know what? We have no idea what Jesus has in store for us when we walk with Him. We have no idea! God does immeasurably more than we could ever imagine or dream if we just choose to let go, surrender, and simply follow Him.

god pours grace over you.

God Lavishes Love on You

When I first started writing this book, it came easy to me. There are so many truths about the Lord that have set my heart free. But as I continued writing, it became harder and harder to let go of the lies in my head and to focus on the truth of Jesus Christ. So I started looking around me—at mundane things like the way I cut an onion, the colors of sunrises, the way my kids learned lessons. I started to become aware of just how much we're surrounded by God's truths.

When we start to retrain our minds to look for God's truths, we start to find them everywhere. We start to know and trust that we have a God who lavishes love on us, pours grace on us, chases after us, holds our hands, and never leaves our side. And, sets our hearts completely free!

DaySpring

LIVE YOUR FAITH

Dear Friend,

This book was prayerfully crafted with you, the reader, in mind—every word, every sentence, every page—was thoughtfully written, designed, and packaged to encourage you...right where you are this very moment. At DaySpring, our vision is to see every person experience the life-changing message of God's love. So, as we worked through rough drafts, design changes, edits and details, we prayed for you to deeply experience His unfailing love, indescribable peace, and pure joy. It is our sincere hope that through these Truth-filled pages your heart will be blessed, knowing that God cares about you—your desires and disappointments, your challenges and dreams.

He knows. He cares. He loves you unconditionally.

BLESSINGS!
THE DAYSPRING BOOK TEAM

Additional copies of this book and
other DaySpring titles can be purchased
at fine bookstores everywhere.
Order online at dayspring.com
or
by phone at 1-877-751-4347